WHAT FEEDS US

ALSO BY DIANE LOCKWARD

Eve's Red Dress
Against Perfection (a chapbook)

What Feeds Us

Diane Lockward

WIND PUBLICATIONS
2006

International Standard Book Number 1893239578
Library of Congress Control Number   2006928890

First edition

The epigraph is from M.F.K. Fisher's "The Gastronomical Me," published in *The Art of Eating,* 50th Anniversary edition, copyright 2004 by M.F.K. Fisher. Reprinted with permission of John Wiley & Sons, Inc.

Cover Art by Brian Rumbolo, www.brianrumbolo.com

Acknowledgments

Grateful acknowledgment is made to the following journals in which some of the poems in this collection first appeared:

Ascent: "Anniversary"

Atlanta Review: "Heart on the Unemployment Line," "The History of Vanilla"

The Barefoot Muse: "Love Test: A Ghazal"

Bryant Literary Review: "A Boy's Bike"

Cider Press Review: "The Tomato Envies the Peach"

Edison Literary Review: "Grief on Schooley Mountain"

Fulcrum: An Annual of Poetry and Aesthetics: "Meditation in the Park"

GSU Review: "Hurricane Season"

The Innisfree Poetry Journal: "Blueberry," "Wren House"

Kalliope: "The Bee Charmer"

The Louisville Review: "After the Ice Storm My Son Does Not Come Home," "A Change in the Air"

Mad Poets Review: "I Find My Man"

Margie: "Gender Issue"

PMS: PoemMemoirStory: "Invective Against the Bumblebee"

Poet Lore: "The Beekeeper," "Linguini"

Poetry Southeast: "Reconstruction"

Prairie Schooner: "Annelida," "Pyromania," "The Summer He Left"

Red Mountain Review: "An Average Day for an Average Liar"

Red Rock Review: "Metamorphoses"

The Seattle Review: "Organic Fruit"

The Spoon River Poetry Review: "The Best Words"

Soundings East: "Insomniac"

Stone Table Review: "You Should Avoid Doctors"

US 1 Worksheets: "The First Artichoke"

Willow Review: "They Weren't June and Ward Cleaver"

"Pyromania" was reprinted in the *Poetry Calendar 2007*, ed. Shafiq
Naz (Alhambra Publishing).

My gratitude goes to all my poet friends who continue to fuel and
support my work. Special thanks to Barbara Crooker, gentle
taskmaster and incomparable fact-checker; to Gina and John
Larkin and Jessica deKoninck, loyal members of the po-group; to
the Frost Place and the Provincetown Fine Arts Work Center, two
places that nourish poets; to Charlie Hughes and Wind Publications
for taking me on in the first place and then sticking with me; to
Brian Rumbolo, my amazing cover artist; and to the New Jersey
State Council on the Arts for the gift of a fellowship.

For my family
Lew
Wes, Coley, and Lacey

Contents

. . . there is nourishment in the heart,
to feed the wilder, more insistent hungers.

—M.F.K. Fisher,
The Gastronomical Me

What Feeds Us

I

I brought the things I really need—
two books I love, a laptop,
clean white paper, a radio
in case I get lonely.
I packed two issues of *The Hungry Mind Review*
and just enough clothes.
Vitamins, ginger tea, a Gauguin cup.
I carried three almond croissants,
one of which I have already eaten.

II

I see a white chocolate chip
macadamia nut cookie in McNulty's Deli,
and right away I start thinking about Joe
and the story he told about Darlene,
the one girl he really could have loved back
in high school, Darlene with the long yummy legs,
when Joe was a short, fat-assed kid
with zits. He'd sit in the cafeteria
and watch luscious Darlene nibble
a cookie, and he'd dream that one day
she'd sashay to his table,
hold out her cookie like a valentine,
and he'd take that cookie, and Darlene's lips
would be all over it.

III

Imagine this: a world
where you could have as many
cheeseburgers and french fries
as you wanted, and the burger
would be the one you really wanted,
red onions, tomatoes, lettuce,
and Russian dressing, and the fries
would arrive hot from the fryer, extra crispy
the way you'd ordered them,
and you could pour on just as much salt
as you wanted and no one would say,
"Hey, that's too much salt—
what are you, a cow or something?"
And the catsup would come out
with one quick tap.

IV

Saturday my father drives us to his garden
out in the country because my brother and I
have been bad. Tall spikes
of gladiolus—peach, pink, purple, and white—
clusters of blossoms, row after row.
This time we do not
go into the garden. This time
we must clear the pile of rusty cans by the barn.
They reek of putrid water.
When we move them,
bees and wasps fly out.
If we cry, we'll be punished.

V

In his dream Darlene looks at Joe
the way Bergman looked at Bogart in *Casablanca*,
and she rises, she rises slowly,
slithers across the room,
and it is just as he'd dreamed it would be:
she holds out one of her yummy cookies,
as if making an offering to a god,
and Joe capitulates, no thinking time at all,
accepts the cookie into his mouth,
and it tastes like love. He nibbles
his way through firm, fine biscuit,
devours it chip by chip.

VI

At the flower show in Marlboro,
my father puts my name
on the flowers he grew
and enters them in the junior competition.
I receive a blue ribbon.
A man standing in front of the flowers says,
"Her father grew these gladiolus.
Who are they kidding?"
I find my father and begin to cry.
I try to find the right words
for shame, but all I can do
is repeat what the man said.
My father puts me in the car, leaves me there all day.
On the way home, he won't stop for food,
though I haven't eaten for hours.
He says crybabies don't eat.

VII

In my story, Eve walked out of the Garden,
unencumbered by Adam
and carrying only the apple.
She didn't know where she was going,
but knew she'd need something to eat.

one

The First Artichoke

Though everyone said no one could grow
artichokes in New Jersey, my father
planted the seeds and grew one magnificent
artichoke, late-season, long after the squash,
tomatoes, and zucchini.

It was the derelict in my father's garden,
little Buddha of a vegetable, pinecone gone awry.
It was as strange as a bony-plated armadillo.

My mother prepared the artichoke as if preparing
a miracle. She snipped the bronzy winter-kissed tips,
mashed breadcrumbs, oregano, parmesan, garlic,
and lemon, stuffed the mush between the leaves,
baked, then placed the artichoke on the table.
This, she said, was food we could eat with our fingers.

When I hesitated, my father spoke of beautiful Cynara,
who'd loved her mother more than she'd loved Zeus.
In anger, the god transformed her
into an artichoke. And in 1949 Marilyn Monroe
had been crowned California's first Artichoke Queen.

I peeled off a leaf like my father did,
dipped it in melted butter, and with my teeth
scraped and sucked the nut-flavored slimy stuff.
We piled up the inedible parts, skeletons
of leaves and purple prickles.

Piece by piece, the artichoke came apart,
the way we would in 1959, the year the flowerbuds

of the artichokes in my father's garden bloomed
without him, their blossoms seven inches wide
and violet-blue as bruises.

But first we had that miracle on our table.
We peeled and peeled, a vegetable striptease,
and worked our way deeper and deeper,
down to the small filet of delectable heart.

The Summer He Left

The lawn filled with dandelions.
Because weeds meant he was gone,
she thought they were beautiful,
a blanket of gold over the green.
Because weeds on grass meant
he wasn't coming back, she was not
afraid. The whole world turned
yellow. No longer cowering
behind the mountain, the sun rose
like Lazarus and warmed the earth.
Marigolds bloomed in the garden.
Sunflowers sprung up like born-again
Christians—lemon lilies, goldenrod,
buttercups, and coreopsis. Bees, dizzy
with temptation of yellow, buzzed
in their velvet tutus. Tiger swallowtails
flapped wings, slow-motion applause.
Goldfinches, orioles, warblers,
not missing blue, jazzed the trees.
At night, the sky streaked with topaz.
The stars, those little cowards, crept out
of their hiding places. Orion lit up
the dark. K-ROCK blared golden oldies,
and she danced to the *Yellow Rose
of Texas* and *Tie a Yellow Ribbon*,
danced like some wild thing,
her straw-colored hair whirling in circles,
the miller's daughter at the wheel,
all around her yellow spinning out gold,
and more gold, not fool's gold, but real.

Gender Issue

George thinks he'd like to play with dolls.
This man loves women but envies girls
their dolls and wants his own, no GI Joe or Ken
but a real girl's doll, Miss Alexander or
Muffy, Ginny, Barbie, or an American Girl.

He dreams of a portmanteau full of doll's clothes,
a purple party dress with hand-smocked bodice
and genuine lace, pajamas with pearl buttons,
black patent leather dancing shoes, and changing her
from swimsuit to gold lamé evening gown.

Most of all he wants a baby doll, not
plastic and hard-edged, but with skin that feels
human. Tiny Tears, Cuddle Baby, or Cabbage Patch.
He does a Google search, orders a baby
off the internet, a modern immaculate conception.

Nights he tucks it snug as an embryo under his shirt,
craves pickles, hot fudge sundaes, buttered popcorn.
Soon the yeasty rising of belly, taut and round
as a drum, shifting and pulsing inside.
His arches collapse, his lower back aches.

In bed he grows restless, flops from side to side.
Electrical charges down the lightning rod of spine.
He breathes and pants—*phh, phh, phh*—as women
on television do, legs bent at the knees, and pushes,
feels the hot rush of water, the salmon-swim of child.

She slides between his legs, a perfect home
delivery. He bathes the petal-soft skin, like any real
mother would, feeds and burps his baby,
strokes the pearls of her toes, remembers
the dancing shoes, and vows to kill the man who harms
this child, pink and delicate as a tea-rose.

The Shampoo Artist:
A Really Dramatic Monologue

Good morning! I'm your shampoo boy.
For this hour, you're my Galatea.
Lean back while I lather you
with an herbal shampoo, scented
with lavender. I massage your scalp, each
artistic finger moving in a circular motion,
goosebumping your flesh. I was born
to give shampoos. This is my life's work.

Imagine you're a marshmallow, plump and spongy.
I could skewer and roast you over a campfire,
press you between graham crackers and
Hershey bars, transform you into a s'more.
You're a puff of snow on bee balm.
A mound of meringue on a pie.
Spores of fluff on a dandelion.

Oh no! A little man's in your tresses,
down on his knees, praying
on top of your brainpan, that same louse
who keeps coming back like seborrhea.
Splat! squashed like a nit and washed
away with the rest of the scurf.
No more static, no split ends, no more heat-
damaged hair, no nights itching and scratching.
You'll never have dandruff again!

And now a conditioner, specially formulated
and emulsified to freshen your follicles.
Breathe in the exotic fruits, a fusion of passion

flower, persimmon, and mango. Let your hair fly free, every strand voluptuous and vibrant, body rejuvenated and lifted. No tangles, knots, or tears. This sink is the altar where I do my work.

Sometimes in Dreams

I woke this morning from a sweet dream of having my hand
held by a stranger. It left me feeling lonely, worse than when
I'd been hurt by my neighbor's dog, Spotty, who'd barked at
me in the stairwell. I've suspected for a long time that Spotty
doesn't like me. No reason for that. I'm usually polite to him.
Yesterday a letter appeared in my mailbox, and I got hopeful
someone had sent tidings or money. It was coupons for stuff
I don't need or want like a clean chimney or a burial plot. I felt
let down as when you bite into an attractive chocolate and find
a date inside after anticipating a cherry or a morsel of apricot.
I told myself I could take it, the way flowers take rain, how they
get beaten down but pop right back up, or the way a lobster
washes onto the beach, turns around and goes straight back
to the sea, or the way a paralyzed man in his dream jumps and
smacks the rim, wakes still in his chair but keeps on dreaming.
It's been years since I've had a genuine date, one that didn't
come from my personal ad—*white female, 36, single, unathletic,*
disliked by dogs, seeks non-smoking male with similar interests.
My neighbor says I'll be kidnapped, raped, or murdered, maybe
all three. Today my hair can't decide if it's red or gold, so I can't
decide what to wear. Ridiculous to have hair that is indecisive.
Mother always said my hair was my primary feature. Maybe it is,
but only because the other features are so dismal. Blue goes
with everything, she said. I've got a closetful of blue. Sometimes
I'm so blue I don't think I'll ever see green again, and the only
man who will ever want me is the one I manufacture in a dream.
Some days I'm grateful to have even him. His voice is gentle
and he tells good jokes, and after he's gone in the morning, my
body remembers everything—the breeze of his breath across
my neck, the taste of his mouth, so soft and sweet at the center.

The Tomato Envies the Peach

The lady of this house is in love
with the peach. How gently she places it
on the sill to catch the shaft of sun.
How many times she passes it under her nose
and breathes. So careful she is
not to bruise it, squeezing between finger and thumb,
coaxing ripeness. Against the furry buttocks,
she presses her lips, leaves the imprint of teeth,
uppers and lowers, like a wreath,

while I who am all firm flesh
and smooth skin languish in the vegetable bin,
sandwiched between the stiff carrot and atrocious
onion. I shrivel and grow soft and must be peeled
and chopped, my seeds cast off,
and am tossed in a pot for sauce, beaten
and most horribly mashed with wooden spoon,
when I would wish to be taken
in her hand, slurped, and eased
down that pearl-white throat.

Love Test: A Ghazal

The sign on the wall read: *Test on Love*
Coming Soon. "My God," I thought, "a test on love!"

I felt the familiar panic,
the tightening in my chest. On love

I'd be lucky if I pulled a C-.
I've always made a mess of love.

It's not as if I haven't tried.
Why, I've even gone in quest of love.

I've studied, done research, pulled all-nighters,
but I can't master the lesson. Love

and its meaning seem to elude me,
though I've given my best to love.

I trembled at the thought of the upcoming exam,
knew I'd never get the gist of love.

What if the teacher called me in front of the class
and made this request: "On love

please speak extemporaneously"?
I'd look like a fool when I confessed, "On love

I can't speak at all." Or worse, an essay question
demanding some new twist on love!

What if it were fill-in-the-blanks that required
memorization of the entire text of love?

What if my answers were stupid or trite,
seemingly given in jest of love?

Maybe I'd get lucky—multiple choice or true and false.
Then at least I could guess on love.

If nothing else worked, I could always throw up
a prayer: "Dear God, let me be blessed in love.

Don't let me suffer the shame of hearing,
Diane, once again, you've received an F in love."

Heart on the Unemployment Line

It's a good heart,
in the midst of the matter,
not dangling on anyone's sleeve.
Previously left in San Francisco.
Experienced being wrenched and hung out to dry.
No daws peck at it now.
Works hard, never skips a beat, shows up on time,
even with throbs and aches, even when sick.
Four-chambered pumping machine the size of a fist.
Pumps its store of blood each day,
always in circulation, making its rounds.
Team player, cooperates with capillaries,
arteries, and veins, all blood-saturated.
A versatile heart, innocent or evil,
sweet or bitter, light, heavy, full, faint, or dear.
Systematic, keeps to a schedule.
Once stolen by a nimble-fingered thief, high
on a hill, later returned.
Occasionally stays up late playing cards,
enjoys the shuffling, the quick flutter,
being held in someone's hand.
Grows fonder during absence,
pours itself out, likes its cockles warm.
Always at the center of things—artichoke,
palm tree, head of lettuce. More reliable than the brain.
This heart won't burn, arrest, attack, or fail.
Once was dropped and broken, sutured by Time.
Never taken a bullet though something like a knife moved through it.
Even in grief, it keeps on beating.

Wren House

My husband hung it
from an S hook, eased the curve
over the evergreen's low-hanging
branch. A slanted roof, a hole
wide enough for the small smooth
body of the wren to push through,
too narrow for squirrels or jays.

We could not bear the possibility of loss.

A hinged door, tiny latch we could open
at season's end to scrape out the nest.

We offered temptation,
a feeder near the house, filled
with seeds. We did everything
right, hoping the wrens would come
and knowing the house needed
to hang long enough to blend,
so no bird would mistake it for a trap.

We knew something about adaptive
coloration. For months, we imagined
the bundle of grass and twigs, eggs
hatching, the fluttering of wings.

We listened for singing.

We had waited like this once before,
wanting some soft creature to fly in.

A Change in the Air

When I came home from school, she wasn't there.
Something in the house said trouble,
said not just *out*, but *gone*.

She left no evidence of having gone,
no notes, no open drawers, just absence in the air,
as if the house were afraid to breathe.

Gone, the house whispered,
gone to a place for women who talk
of killing themselves.

I had never seen my mother cry, not even
when my father left with his beautiful mistress.
Now she wanted to die.

She came back in spring, but different.
Shock treatments left her stupid for days,
days when she couldn't move.

She was like the doll I'd once dropped
who'd gone to the doll hospital and come home
with eyelids that no longer opened and closed.

I cared for her as I had my broken doll,
like a new mother who is always afraid—
if she doesn't do this right, her child might die.

Thirty years later when for a second time the air
changed and I was no longer anyone's mother,
I remembered how my mother had broken
and finally forgave her.

two

Blueberry

Deep-blue hue of the body, silvery bloom
on its skin. Undersized runt of a fruit,
like something that failed to thrive, dented top
a fontanel. Lopsided globe. A temperate zone.
Tiny paradox, tart and sweet, homely
but elegant afloat in sugar and cream,
baked in a pie, a cobbler, a muffin.

The power of blue. Number one antioxidant fruit,
bantam-weight champ in the fight against
urinary tract infections, best supporting actor
in a fruit salad. No peeling, coring, or cutting.
Lay them out on a counter, strands of blue pearls.
Pop one at a time, like M&M's, into your mouth.
Be a glutton and stuff in a handful, your tongue,
lips, chin dyed blue, as if feasting on indigo.
Fruit of the state of New Jersey.
Favorite fruit of my mother.

Sundays she scooped them into pancake batter,
poured circles onto the hot greased griddle, sizzled
them gold and blue, doused with maple syrup.

This is what I want to remember: my mother
and me, our quilted robes, hair in curlers,
that kitchen, *that* table,
plates stacked with pancakes, blueberries sparkling
like gemstones, blue stars in a gold sky,
the universe in reverse,
the two of us eating blueberry pancakes.

After the Ice Storm
My Son Does Not Come Home

Hours after he stormed out, wind knocks
ice off the roof, startles me awake.
2 AM—light under the door. Not home,
and I'd said no later than midnight.

I practice deep breathing, natural tranquilizer,
five counts in, hold it in the diaphragm,
let it out slowly, repeat five times, relax, and go back
to a sleep without dreams.

It's been so long since I've dreamed,
I'd be grateful now for even that old one
where I show up someplace important, take off my coat,
and I'm in panties and bra, or worse, naked.

And I'm still wondering if he'll be okay,
if he'll ever find his way home,
if maybe I'll be happy when I'm old,
and if I can wait that long.

Hours later I wake and see the first crocus
pushing purple through the sheen of ice.
A day of lifting towards the light,
the delicate petals unfolding.

I want it to be like that for him—
sunlight, the wind will stop blowing,
and he'll find his way home.

Invective Against the Bumblebee

Escapee from a tight cell, yellow-streaked,
sex-deprived sycophant to a queen,
you have dug divots in my yard
and like a squatter trespassed in my garage.

I despise you for you have swooped down
on my baby boy, harmless on a blanket of lawn,
his belly plumping through his orange stretch suit,
yellow hat over the fuzz of his head.
Though you mistook him for a sunflower,
I do not exonerate you,
for he weeps in my arms, trembles, and drools,
finger swollen like a breakfast sausage.
Now my son knows pain.
Now he fears the grass.

Fat-assed insect! Perverse pedagogue!
Henceforth, may flowers refuse to open for you.
May cats chase you in the garden.
I want you shellacked by rain, pecked by shrikes,
mauled by skunks, paralyzed by early frost.
May farmers douse your wings with pesticide.
May you never again taste the nectar
of purple clover or honeysuckle.
May you pass by an oak tree just in time
to be pissed on by a dog.

And tomorrow may you rest on my table
as I peruse the paper. May you shake
beneath the scarred face of a serial killer.
May you be crushed by the morning news.

Annelida

My husband is saving the worms again.
All night, heavy rain, now the driveway crawls
with worms, afraid of drowning, but so dumb
they will broil to death in the sun, except
for my husband who picks them up,
one by one, places them on the still-wet grass,
then drives to work without even washing
his hands. I imagine him in his office sniffing
his fingers for the earthy scent of worms,

and I remember being 6 and loving
worms, collecting them in a *worm bin*,
a five-pound pickle bucket, so I understand
his affection. I filled my bin with a bedding
of peat moss and soil, soaked and squeezed it
by hand, punctured breathing holes in the lid.

I took a trowel into the garden and dug
for worms. Pink, gray, and reddish-brown.
The long fat ones I loved best, the way they shrunk
and stretched when touched. The way they reared
their heads. I fed them chicken mash, decayed leaves,
and kitchen waste. I wanted my worms to live.

No eyes, no ears, no backbone, no legs.
Each a tube inside a tube, like a knife in a sheath.
Hermaphroditic. Conjoined by a slime tube.
My worms multiplied. I imagined the five pairs
of hearts, their blood, red like mine.

This was nothing to do with sex—I was 6!
This was tactile, olfactory. I wanted the feel, the smell
of worms in my hands, on my skin.
Sometimes I lay down on the floor and let worms
crawl across my belly. Once I put a worm in my mouth.

When I was 7, I upended the bin and freed
the worms, imagined them sliding
through the earth, finding their way home.
Some days I can hardly wait until my husband
comes home, and puts his hands on my skin.

The History of Vanilla

Need something to lull you to sleep?
This could be the sedative you long for,
hedge against loneliness, antidote
to grief, the bean of your desire.
Discrete at wrist and neck, keepers
of the secrets of vanilla. Listen and doze:
Totonacos, Aztecs, Hernando Cortez.
Whisper his name. Precious plunder
of Spain. With cacao, elixir rich and noble.
Drift into dreamy exotica, Madagascar,
Mexico, Tahiti. Picture the orchid, hand-
pollinated, the dangling fruit. Rootlets
attached to trees and vines. You, unrooted,
rootless, uprooted, always on snooze
alarm. Latin root: *vagina*. Diminutive
of *vaina*: sheath, vagina, pod.
Pods bundled in blankets, laid in the sun,
wrapped back up to sweat
overnight as you so often do.
Repeat and repeat until properly cured,
until the slow, gentle recirculation
of menstruum moves through your beans,
until you're pure. Pure vanilla extract,
perfect for anything you crave, savory
soups and sauces, vanilla-seared scallops,
lamb peppered and roasted in creamy
bourbon vanilla, ice cream bean-pricked.
Soporific of your dreams. A kitchen,
an island, a man, the two of you making
crème brûlée, the air laced with fragrant
oily liquid, the ripe pod in your hand.

An Average Day for an Average Liar

The average person tells thirteen lies each day.
—Dr. Georgia Witkin

One, on a day much like any other, I awake with alarm
clock blaring, turn to you, and say, "Your face
is no longer imprinted on my heart."

Two, I aim a dart to the groin, say I've taken a *paramour*.

Three, he's a man who loves
to build things, handles the adze, hammer, and awl—
his muscular arms, laden with 2 x 4's, an aphrodisiac.

Four, I say he lives under the cover
of the Witness Protection Program, his name a secret.

Five, he smokes a pipe and smells like figs.

Six, I say he's a gymnast
in bed, master of every position in the *Karma Sutra*,
knows what a *yoni* is and brings it to blossom.

Seven, I praise his intellect, list books he's read—
Remembrance of Things Past and all twelve volumes
of *Dance to the Music of Time* which you once insisted
could only be done if one were sentenced to life
in prison, no possibility of parole.

Eight, his sense of humor coruscates. He juggles
double-entendres, scorns puns, perceives irony, relishes
repartée, never steals a punch line, cherishes my bon mots.

Nine, he pens novels of Russian proportions, is adored
by the *literati,* writes poetry, too, his last collection
favorably reviewed by William Logan.

Ten, he's slender, a man of sartorial splendor,
whose every garment I've memorized—his blue jeans,
each turtleneck, tank, and tee, every sock in his drawer,
and his hiking boots in which he does not walk
but strides like a man on a mission.

Eleven, he hates watching sports on tv, prefers to toss
a salad, knows every kind of lettuce.

Twelve, each morning in our special hotel he brings me
one perfect pastry from the *pâtisserie.* He bites
from one end, I the other, the custard between us sweet
as French kisses, our tongues foraging like bees
in blossoms, our faces plastered with chocolate.

Thirteen, I turn off the lights and recant, swear
I made him up, fingers crossed behind my back.
I produce tears and fall upon your chest,
and confess, and confess, and confess.

Meditation on Green

It comes to me as a commandment:
Thou shalt meditate on green.
And because I am obedient,
my thoughts turn to grass, blades
crushed under my feet, tiny green
grasshopper grinding his broken song.
Thence to the lime for it is a tart
fruit and hangs from trees without
causing any woman to fall. Green
for the novice, the inexperienced,
the not-knowing-any-better.
The pickle, repeatedly tempting me
to devour its green obscene shape.
So many vegetables—peas, beans,
celery, broccoli, asparagus—emerge
from dirt, yet the earth yields the emerald,
color of my last lover's eyes. For him
I wore a dress of emerald satin.
Green the color of money, sound
of some other woman's voice.
Signal for *Go* or *Come*. Frogs, algae, and scum.
Lichen, moss, mold, parrots, toads, iguanas.
My lizard-green lover, turning and turning—
him I now curse: May his hair turn green
as in the movie I saw when I was a girl,
The Boy with Green Hair. All summer
I dreamed of that boy, as now I conjure
potions to send my lover—to turn him green,
the color of contagion, burn him in bile, feed him
seedless green grapes, skin peeled with the blade
of my Swiss army knife, to offer one gelatinous

globe—*Here, eat this!* Oh! to watch him pluck
the head from its stake, swallow it whole, fall and
fall, and choke on that green grape of sorrow,
twist and shrivel with despair, tongue
darting and hissing, unable to speak.

Metamorphoses

A good teacher carries a torch.
                —Lecture Notes, English Education Methods

1

I watch the boy in my class fall in love.
He waits at his locker with assumed nonchalance
until he spots the girl, then drifts to my room
and follows her in. He's dropped his slouch,
switched to contacts, snazzed his hair. And I know
that won't matter. She's way too cool for him.

He no longer dismisses poetry, wants
to resuscitate pastorals and aubades.
He learns by heart from *Romeo and Juliet*:
"O, she doth teach the torches to burn bright.
It seems she hangs upon the cheeks of night
like a rich jewel in an Ethiop's ear."
He gazes at the girl with such longing,
I sizzle and burn with remembered heat.

2

By second semester, I'm making lesson plans
with him in mind: We act scenes from *Othello*,
read tales from Ovid. He pays attention
during *Jane Eyre,* audibly sighs when the hero
gets the girl, though some guys say Rochester's
a jerk, and it's just sappy chick lit anyhow.

We spend all of April on sonnet sequences
and the tradition of amorous verse.
I lecture on Petrarch and Laura, Dante
and Beatrice, Shakespeare's Dark Lady.
He takes notes as if writing the combination
to the vault holding the treasure he seeks.

Outside, cherry trees fill with pink blossoms.
Honeysuckle and lilacs perfume the air.

3

Tiny buds sprout from my shoulders.
Soon I can no longer sleep on my back.
I fold the cumbersome wings under a sweater,
hide bow and arrows in my briefcase.

In June I see them strolling the hallway,
arms threaded together. Astrophel and Stella
enter the room. Stars light up the ceiling.
Gold dust rains from fluorescent fixtures.

From the back row, Shakespeare, Rochester,
and a whole gang of lovers cheer him on.
I close the door, hold in all that light.
Once more, I read from *Amoretti*, stunned

by my own remarkable powers, my entire
body electric, my hands carrying fire.

You Should Avoid Doctors

Because they find something you don't
want. That's their job, finding trouble. They impose
music you'd never choose, a paper gown, a cold room,
then force you to disrobe and uncover
information you've hidden for years—
you're overweight, or under, need more exercise,
less caffeine, and everything you love
is dangerous. You've never been this exposed.

You cough and breathe, cough and breathe.
They listen to your heart, a cold disk placed
on chest and back, alarm on their faces, suspicious
of this and that, as if your heart were a criminal,
which often it is.

                 They misread the flutters, leaps,
and flips as disease—myocardial infarction,
atrial fibrillation, endocarditis—when you know deep
in your heart that it's fear you feel and you awake each day
not with joy but despair, heartachy, heartsick, heartbroken,
like some cheesy country western song.

                        So what
can a doctor do? Cut it, stitch it,
repair it? Reach in his fist and rip out
the organ? It's already gone. And the pain
you feel is the phantom kind as when
a leg's blown off after stepping
on a landmine, and even years later the fugitive
limb still throbs to the beat.

Fear

I'm the thing that lurks under the bed
at night, darts out like a snake,
and bites your toes.
                    I'm wasps
poised over your head, abuzz
while you sleep, or don't sleep.
Your neighbor's Doberman pinscher,
loose in the street, teeth crunching
bone.
          I'm the milkman delivering
the bloody girl home.
                    Your mother
leaving again, car rounding
the corner, crumpled face in the mirror,
arm out the window—*Goodbye, goodbye.*
Look at the child, wild-eyed, down
the block—*Don't go, don't go.*
                    Remember
the Schwinn, the hurtle downhill, you,
hurled across asphalt onto your face,
the shrill scream of your voice—
Daddy, Daddy.
                    Your father, his hands
in giant proportions, the pebbles pried
out of your skin.
          Subway system,
platform's edge, a stranger in sweat pants,

closer and closer, his arms outstretched.
Doorbell, hospital, and cops on the phone
nights your son doesn't come home.
Midnight, 3 AM, and 4, paws scratching
walls.
       My mother nicknamed me
depression, anxiety attacks, and panic.
A Xanax nightmare, you awake, crying.
I'm the screech of tires, slam of brakes,
skateboard in front of wheels.
                  Creaks
in dark stairwells, a rock stuck in your cheek,
I'm the bone that won't heal.

Insomniac

Because I could not sleep, I counted
injustices. Back to an army base, to my father,
rigid in uniform during the war,
to the exact moment my brother broke
bottles on concrete, and told me to walk
across glass, barefoot and bloodless,
like the Indian holy man we'd seen in a film.

Because I could not sleep, I replayed 1958,
Fourth of July, Father forcing me into bed
long before dark—I had rolled down
the hill of his lawn. Prisoner locked in my room,
I imagined starbursts, heard lights in the sky—
explosions like dynamite, explosions like bombs.

Because I could not sleep, I remembered
summer, the year my mother left me
alone with my father—bathroom door, broken lock,
sixty days and sixty nights I would not bathe,
skin grown thick as a lizard's with grime.

Because I could not sleep, I went all the way
back to Ohio, to the sleep-away camp
my father said would fix a girl like me,
day after day thrown by a horse named Star,
so many hands high and so many pounds,
the weight of his foot pressing mine.

I could not sleep because sin entered the scene,
the evidence I planted against my brother—
hot water bottle scrawled with his name in black ink—

and when he denied the crime,
the sound of my father's hand pounding on skin,
the sound of my brother breaking.

All night I lay awake remembering once more
a sidewalk in South Carolina, hot and hard,
my father running toward me, always in slow motion,
always carrying me home, how he laid me
on the kitchen table as if I were Abraham's child,
how he sponged me in cool water, and tweezed
shards of glass from my bloody feet.

three

They Weren't June and Ward Cleaver

My parents warned me
if I ate one more pickle,
I would turn into one.
I made an art of licking each pickle
with my little pink tongue—
to stop the dripping, I said,
but really so if anyone wanted
a bite, I could say, *Oh no,*
this pickle's been licked.
This pickle's been in my mouth.
When my belly was filled with dills,
I poured the juice into a tumbler
and joined the grownups for cocktails.

Mother smoked her glamorous cigarettes
and made tiny circles with her highball, amber
whiskey swirling, ice cubes clinking.
Her hair was the color of summer wheat,
and she smelled like lilies of the valley.
Billie Holiday was singing a blue song.
Mother clicked the tune with scarlet nails
and blew smoke rings like signals for war
or help. Father fanned the air and counted
mother's drinks.

On a footstool between them,
I sipped and sipped. No one noticed me
turning green, dill weed powdering my skin,
the small protrusions like pimples or warts.
The room closed around me, glass walls
held me in. I floated in brine. The ceiling

dropped over my head. I could not unscrew
the lid. If I moved, something would shatter.
I waited for my parents to rescue me, to turn me back
to a girl, waited for them to say, *We told you so!*

Someone put me in the fridge.
I've lived here now for years, grown used to the dark,
the occasional light, comfortable among outcast onions,
broccoli, and the days-old stew. I barely remember
being a girl, or the scent of my mother's perfume.

Organic Fruit

I want to sing
a song worthy of
the avocado, renegade
fruit, strict individualist, pear
gone crazy. Praise to its skin

like an armadillo's, the refusal
to adulate beauty. Schmoo-shaped
and always face forward, it is what it
is. Kudos to its courage, its inherent love
of democracy. Hosannas for its motley coat,
neither black, brown, nor green, but purple-hued,
like a bruise. Unlike the obstreperous coconut, the

avocado yields to the knife, surrenders its hide of leather,
blade sliding under the skin and stripping the fruit. Praise
to its nakedness posed before me, homely, yellow-green,
and slippery, bottom-heavy like a woman in a Renoir, her
flesh soft velvet. I cup the fruit in my palm, slice and hold,
slice and hold, down to the stone at the core, firm fist at the
center. Pale peridot crescents slip out, like slivers of moon.
Exquisite moment of ripeness! a dash of salt, the first bite
squishes between tongue and palate, eases down my

throat, oozes vitamins and oil. Could anything be more
delicious, more digestible? Plaudits to its versatility,
yummy in Cobb salad, saucy in guacamole, boldly
stuffed with crabmeat. My avocado dangles from
a tree, lifts its puckered face to the sun, pulls
all that light inside. Praise it for being small,
misshapen, and durable. Praise it for
the largeness of its heart.

The Beekeeper

When the bee flies into my lunch bag
and Ann puts in her hand to coax him out,
I'm already back at Red Raider Camp watching
two girls covered with bees from a nest
they'd unearthed, both girls screaming, doing
some kind of dance, arms flapping and
swatting, the two of them singing a chorus
of *Help Me*'s, the rest of us campers standing there,
terrified, fascinated, sorry for the girls, but glad
it wasn't us, not able to help, maybe
not wanting to help because we didn't like
those girls, their pasty faces and sausage sandwiches,
and we were mesmerized as the velvet tide of yellow
moved up their arms, their faces, their eyes, stinging
them again and again, until finally the counselor yelled,
Run! Jump in the lake!, and the girls did, and
it was over, except for the crying and the welts lifting
their skin in pink puffs.
                                    When Ann slips
her hand deep into the bag and charms
the bee, I'm back in the nightmare of my childhood, bees
swarming the ceiling of my bedroom, waiting for me
to sleep, thousands of bees in military rows,
an army of bees, their lances, spears, and bayonets
pointed at me, soldiers patiently waiting
for the buzz of my breathing.

I Find My Man

I dream about him, night after night,
imagine myself taking him down,
a let's-get-this-scum-off-the-streets kind of guy,
America's Most Wanted.

It's late night, a convenience store—sometimes
a 7-Eleven, sometimes a Wawa, once a Krauszer's.
I'm buying Cherry Garcia or Chunky Monkey
when I spot him shoplifting beef jerky—

the face seen on posters everywhere,
features memorized by heart—ears, cheeks,
the felonious lips.
I know the missing tip of his index finger.

I wait while he lights a cigarette, wanting him
vulnerable. The cop inside me forces his arms
to the wall, frisks chest and thighs,
pats down the crotch.

A strip search uncovers the tell-tale tattoo,
left shoulder, a snake and the name
of some other girl. *Smack!* with my nightstick—
the satisfying crack of a rib or two.

He calls me *Baby, Baby,* and begs
for mercy, the way I used to do.
I cuff him, hog-tie him, make him incapable
of resisting —

Don't mess with me, Mister.
You've been arrested by the wrong
kind of girl, the kind who goes after the bad guy
and nabs him every time.

Orchids

They are hot and moist in operation, under the
dominion of Venus, and provoke lust exceedingly.
—The British Herbal Guide, 1653

Such flowers must be used with discretion.
Love of them becomes obsession.

A man pursues an orchid as he once
pursued a green-eyed woman. He hunts

in Florida swamps, Thailand, and Brazil,
delirious with lust, blissed on the smell

of dust and mulch, steamy veil of moisture,
breathing pores on leaves, tessellated lure

of waxy sepals, pouched lips, and tubers,
stamen and pistil twisted together,

inflorescence of *Phalaenopsis,*
Vanda Sanderiana, Cryptanthus.

Dream-haunted nights—ghost, slipper, and spider,
the deep plunge to the nectar inside her.

Linguini

It was always linguini between us.
Linguini with white sauce, or
red sauce, sauce with basil snatched
from the garden, oregano rubbed between
our palms, a single bay leaf adrift amidst
plum tomatoes. Linguini with meatballs,
sausage, a side of brascioli. Like lovers
trying positions, we enjoyed it every way
we could—artichokes, mushrooms, little
neck clams, mussels, and calamari—linguini
twining and braiding us each to each.
Linguini knew of the kisses, the smooches,
the *molti baci*. It was never spaghetti
between us, not cappellini, nor farfalle,
vermicelli, pappardelle, fettucini, perciatelli,
or even tagliarini. Linguini we stabbed, pitched,
and twirled on forks, spun round and round
on silver spoons. Long, smooth, and always
al dente. In dark trattorias, we broke crusty panera,
toasted each other—*La dolce vita!*—and sipped
Amarone, wrapped ourselves in linguini,
briskly boiled, lightly oiled, salted, and lavished
with sauce. *Bellissimo, paradisio, belle gente!*
Linguini witnessed our slurping, pulling, and
sucking, our unraveling and raveling, chins
glistening, napkins tucked like bibs in collars,
linguini stuck to lips, hips, and bellies, cheeks
flecked with *formaggio*—parmesan, romano,
and shaved pecorino—strands of linguini flung
around our necks like two fine silk scarves.

Meditation in the Park

I was sitting on a hunk of granite,
heaved up by the earth, or maybe
unearthed by a steam shovel when somebody
was building something. Stuff like that
intrigues me. Where things come from.
Where they go when they go away.
This rock wasn't comfortable, but it had flecks
of silver that held my attention. Pretty, like little mirrors.
Nothing I could see my face in, but I didn't want
to see my face because I'd been crying again,
sitting in the park thinking about things that got lost,
that went away when I wasn't looking, when I wasn't careful.
Like my old boyfriend and my dog, Penny the Dachshund.
My mother said she got gobbled up by a steam shovel,
the driver mistaking her for a log.
And Kiki the Siamese Cat disappeared for weeks—
I thought she was dead—but she came back,
pregnant! Her six kittens died of disease, each
stiffening as if stretching, then gone for good.
When my father left for good, my mother lost her head,
closed herself in a room like Houdini squeezing into a box.
She came back too, but no longer
my mother, more like a jackrabbit ready to run.
My friend Jessica says she won't let herself fall in love
with her socks because eventually one will get lost.
I understand that kind of thinking. But I want to love
two at a time. When one gets lost, I'll still
have the other. Sometimes when I sit in the park,
I find things, things that somebody else lost,
somebody who's feeling sad somewhere else, maybe
finding my stuff and wondering what the heck

to do with it. To the finder it's just somebody's junk.
To the loser it's special, except it's gone.
Like the amethyst ring that fell off my finger in sixth grade
and got me in trouble with my father because I wasn't
allowed to wear it. It had a band of antique gold and a stone
like a Concord grape that made me wonder, What's the point
of something that beautiful, that purple left in a box?

Reconstruction

I am a house he would move into,
so framed for this man. With hammer
and nails he holds me together,
such tools he carries, his pliers, his adze,
gives me his awl, his drill and bits.
He puts a roof over my head.
I am shingled and waterproofed,
plumbed, mitered, and wired. He makes
of me a dream house, a cream puff,
my rough-hewn timber smoothed.
Broom-clean, in move-in condition.
I am two-storied now. He builds a fire in me.

The Gift

Christmas morning, gifts under the tree.
One for you, long and heavy.
Remove bows, foil, and lid.
Inside lies a child, a boy, seventeen.
He's your new son.

Like so many gifts, the Prodigal Boy Kit
requires partial assembly. Easy, if you follow
directions. First, lay out the pieces—
arms and legs on the floor, now the head.
Do not open the bag of organs yet.
Next, attach limbs to torso,
using the screws and bolts.
A lug wrench is enclosed for convenience.
Tighten and tighten until your arms ache.
Quite a handsome boy, don't you think?

Insert the organs and take your time.
They're color-coded for ease of assembly.
Of course, and wouldn't you know it,
though the attached certificate asserts
Lila Watkins inspected the kit
at our Michigan plant prior to shipment,
essential pieces are missing.
There's no tongue. This boy won't speak.
And no brain will ever go where a brain ought to be.
Look at the irreplaceable heart, already broken.
Batteries—eight double A's—not included,
and Christmas morning, nothing's open,
not even the 7-Eleven. This boy won't run.

Maybe it's better this way.
See how nicely he sits at the table.
This boy can't get in trouble, won't stir
in his sleep, won't ever turn
eighteen. He'll last forever.
This boy's durable.
This boy won't break.

Undone Triolet

Things begun but left unfinished:
pregnancy without a child,
melted virga, the tale half-told,
sentence forever unfinished,
paintings abandoned by da Vinci,
San Xavier's tower untolled,
music Schubert left unfinished,
pregnancy without a child.

Grief on Schooley Mountain

The cancer had come back,
this time in his stomach.

Her voice calling his name
filled the air. Huge rocks and stones,
no longer implacable, crumbled.

The wolf lay down with the rabbit
and wept. The fox curled up in bed
and could not move for days.
The grizzly, awake after his long
sleep and hearing the news,
returned to his cave and prayed
for a longer winter.

Blight spread throughout the woods,
bark peeled away, tumorous knots disfigured
the trunks, and rain so heavy the roots
floated loose, as if the earth
could not keep them down.

In the days between knowing
and not knowing, every living thing
circled the house. All prayed for a miracle:
Could he come back a second time?
The trees he so loved stretched their branches
as if to lift him from his pain. The mountain
cradled him. And the wind held his name.

Showdown with the King Bee

1. I Look in His Face

You come to me in nightmares,
huge and hairy, hanging over my bed,
waiting for me to sleep.

I dream of the sleep-over at Red Raider camp,
girls covered with bees they'd unearthed.
They screamed and screamed. Bees
crawled over them, stung them
again and again, the girls never
so alive as at that moment.

5:30 AM.
I woke from my nightmare, saw gray, thought rain.
Later, sunlight under the shade.
The bell tolled though not seven times,
faint and far away.
Dew on my shoes as I crossed your courtyard,
tang of the air, crisp and pure.

2. I Free-Associate

Crisp—Christmas—Lake Erie—
my grandmother's house—
the year my father wasn't there
because he'd left with his Kim Novak
look-alike mistress.
A gift from him under the tree,
the cashmere sweater

he'd said I couldn't have
because cashmere would ruin me.

3. I Face Facts

All my life I have been afraid:
my father, his hands,
phone calls, novocaine, dogs,
cavities, doctors, the buzzing of bees,
their horrible stingers, the piercing of flesh.
I am still afraid of the dark.

4. I Provide Some History

No news at all on the radio—
the world goes on without me—
only rock 'n' roll, golden oldies—
Won't you let me take you on a   sea cruise?

William Bradford sailed across the sea,
bringing a sense of history, of destiny,
and standing behind him, like a shadow, his wife,
Dorothy, their son back home in Holland.
Off the coast of a new world, Dorothy slipped
over the edge. Too late to save her.

When the clock strikes one, and two, and three,
I'm dancing with Kenny Tredinnick
at Marilyn Stringer's sweet sixteen,
Elvis singing, *Love me tender, love me true,*
and I'm wanting Kenny
to pull me close, his head against mine,

his arms around my waist,
mine around his neck, so afraid
no boy will ever love me.

Blow out the candles and make a wish:
I wish my child would be okay.
I'm afraid he will die.

5. I Face My Fears

Bees are buzzing now, there's danger.
Stingers out, they're looking for meat.
I could not tell my story to anyone but the bees.
Don't circle in too close.

Why do you torment me?
Do you sense my fear?
Does it make you feel big, powerful?
If you sting me, you will die.
Are you symbolic, are you phallic?
Does it give you pleasure to know
I have honey on toast most mornings?
Did you know I lived in that house
when you built your nest under the porch?
Long before I saw you, I heard you inside the walls.

The ceiling slants inward
on two sides, blue
walls up to the flat part, then white.
This is the world
upside down.

Someday I will think about home,
the long ride back, who I'll be
when I get there, and if I'll make
any wrong turns.

6. My Time Is Up

When I finish spilling my guts,
the King Bee says: *I choose you
because you are afraid.*

four

Seduction

Peculiar, the way it starts out small,
then swells to a big fat bottom cupped
in my hand. I wish I could love it,
but something there is about a pear
I can't embrace—that stem popping up
like an exclamation point forcing excitement,
the texture of the skin, not velvety like the peach
or apricot, nor burnished like a cherry or plum,
and the grittiness of the flesh inside.

               I cannot love a man
who loves the pear; yet you attempt seduction,
cajoling like a courtier: *Whatever can be done*
with an apple can be done with a pear.
Anjou, Bartlett, and Bosc—rose-red, lime-green,
russet-toned, and crimson-freckled—
you poach, sauté, and stew, simmer
in sauces and chutney, slice and spice in a pie.
You place your pear in a blender and whip it
into a smoothie. Like an auctioneer at Sotheby's,
you trace its provenance from the volcanic soil
of Washington to a farmer's market in New Jersey.

               Though I refuse to taste
your pear, you appeal to my desire for physical
fitness, displaying your fruit and boasting
of its potassium and vitamin C. Cholesterol, none.
Calories, a minimal 100. You ply me
with dietary fiber. And now a basket spilling
gourmet pears from Harry and David,
each lovingly wrapped in foil, filling the air
with the redolence of pear.

The Best Words

The ones that sound obscene but aren't,
that put a finger to the flame but don't burn.
Words like asinine, poppycock, titmouse, tit for tat,
woodpecker, pecorino, poop deck, and beaver.

In tenth grade Mr. Mungonest, my English teacher,
called Barney Feeley a *young dastard* and silenced
the room. *Dastard!* I was seduced by words that flirt
with danger but don't end up in bed. The threat
of Shylock's *If you prick us, do we not bleed?*

And fructify—I wanted to conjugate
that sinuous verb, like Proteus, changing its form,
oozing into fructuous, assuming the official ring
of fructification, advocating like a president's wife
for the Fructification of America.

Wild words that shake their hips, thrust out their genitalia,
and say, *Feast on this.* Sexagesima—my God!
what a word for the second Sunday before Lent.
Sextuplicate, the versatility of it—noun, verb, adjective—
always occurring six times. And on the equator, positioned
just south of the Sickle of Leo, the constellation Sextans.

My twelfth grade English teacher was Mrs. Cox.
We could not get enough of her name. We raised
our hands and called, *Mrs. Cox, Mrs. Cox, choose me!*
until we drove her out of school swearing
to become a secretary or a nun, but not until we'd fallen
in love with Edmund the Bastard.

Cockatiel, cockatoo—words with wings.
The hoarfrost of winter, lure of a crappie,
handful of nuts, kumquat, lavender crystals of kunzite,
the titillation of shiftless and schist, the bark and bite
of shittimwood, music of sextillion and cockleshells.

And always somewhere in the distance, Jerry Lee Lewis,
blond curls flapping, groin pumping, fingers pounding
the keyboard, his throat belting out *Great balls of fire!*—
words like fat radishes burning my tongue.

Cold Pizza

*You know it's over when you can no longer
bear to watch him eat.*
　　　—Marriage Counselor

Snow dusted the pizza
my husband carried home.
He stomped in cursing, *God damn
snow all over the box!* I pacified him, promised
snow would do no harm, though I wondered why
he hadn't brushed it off instead of complaining
about the weather, the jerk at the pizza shop,
and snow all over his god damn car seat.

Inside the box, our pie waited for someone
to lift the lid. Oregano joined hands with mozzarella
and tomato sauce, and tried to stay warm, indifferent
to the troubles of me and my husband.

My husband's the kind of man who allows his wife
to shovel snow, so I shoveled it into the sink,
and offered a beer. It was Friday night, our night to love
and honor pizza and beer. *God damn right!* he said,
popped the cap with his callused thumb, and toasted
our health. He grabbed the first slice, folded and cracked
the crust as he'd seen real Italians do, and he bit.
Olive oil slipped down his chin, greased the napkin
tucked in his shirt. Two mushrooms plopped in his lap.
His mustache dangled strands of cheese like icicles.

I took a bite of my own slice, worried about the wind
gusting, the cacophony of chewing, slurping,

and gulping, the blizzard brewing in the sink. I sunk
my teeth into cold arctic blue, snow aswirl in drifts, a foot
of it piled between us, the ice in the sink breathing me in.

Virga

Snow that never hits the ground,
as if changing its mind midair.
Strange attribute of weather
when cold meets warm and disappears.
A kind of melting, like the heart grieving without tears.
Something like a hand frozen
in a photograph,
a hand forever waving
goodbye. Sleight of hand, a cheap magician's trick,
the handkerchief tucked behind the ear.
Now you see it, now you don't.
Nothing out of something.
The miller's daughter's gold unspun,
spider's thread of silk lowered and lifted,
the fly left to fly away. A thought unfinished.
Someone you loved almost here. Then vanished.

A Boy's Bike

One morning a bike appears in our driveway,
at the end where we can't not notice it, where
someone who's not being careful will crush it.
A boy's bike, lying on its side like a wounded
animal, black, with green neon streamers
on the handlebars, a well-worn bike with rusty
chain, broken kickstand. It's not our bike, and
we don't want it. We phone the police to ask
if anyone's reported a missing bike. No one has,
and the cop doesn't care about the bike. Maybe
he has crimes to deal with. Things disappearing,
not bikes appearing. We can't throw it in the trash.
We know that somewhere a boy is missing
his bike. Maybe he'll search here and pedal away.
Problem solved. But days go by and no boy
shows up. We begin to worry about the missing
boy. And so it is that our worries double. And then
they triple for we are missing him, and we don't
even know him, but maybe we know a boy like him,
a boy who once lived here, a boy who once took
his sister's new Schwinn without permission, sped
down a hill, and fell, the pedal slashing the back
of his ankle, and he limped home, raised his foot,
and said, *Look, Mom!* a slice so clean no blood yet,
the bone inside white as cuttlefish, and later stitches
and pain. Lesson learned: If you take a bike without
permission, you get hurt. Somewhere a mother hurts;
she is missing her boy. Somewhere a boy hurtles
downhill, out of control, hands off the handles, brakes
failing, spokes of the wheels spinning like silver
plates, and he calls, *Look, Mom!* his face flashing by

so fast we can't see him, but we know this boy
is our boy, and we are there waiting for him to hit
the point of impact, longing for him to find his way
home, to come to us with his bloodless wounds.

Anniversary

Tonight, on this darkest night of the year,
after a satisfying meal,
we will eat *bocconi dolci*.
We will not speak of sadness.
We will not remember.
The antique clock will stop tolling.
For once the chimes will be still.
For this one night only,
earth will defy gravity,
and turn the other way.
I will slice *bocconi dolci*,
place it on pale bone china.
We will be ravenous
for meringue, the three shells
piled on top of each other,
for the cream I whipped,
the ripe strawberries picked
from our garden. The buds
on our tongues will blossom
under delicate layers of chocolate.
And if the doorbell rings, we will not answer.
We will dance until we are dizzy.
We will dance as if we were young,
but quietly, quietly,
as if somewhere in the house
a small child slept,
a child who might be wakened by laughter.

Hurricane Season

Films of dense tissue swirling like storm clouds.
Specks of light inside, and at the center, a fibroid,
glistening like the lodestar that led the Wise Men
to Jesus. Microcalcification, cluster, fibroadenosis—
words with the force of hurricane winds—
cyst, lump, mass.

Warnings on the screen: a hurricane pounding
the coast. Isabel, like my friend's daughter.
People in North Carolina taping window panes,
boarding up homes. Wind so fierce it rips
a building from its foundation,
picks up a woman and hurls her onto concrete.

Ultrasound, MRI. A file on me now, stored
in a basement, as if I were a secret agent or a spy.
Words from a book on torture:
aspiration, fine needle, thick needle, core
biopsy, the rack of a stereotactic table. A list
of possibilities: stage 1, 2, 3, or 4;
mild pain, moderate pain, extreme pain.

A swath of heavy rain from Cape Fear
to the South Santee River. Whirling confusion
of sand pelting, cars fleeing. Radar. Doppler scan.
Category 5, 4, 3, 2. Satellite photos—
Isabel swirling, a mass on the screen,
eye at the center like a nipple.

Days of waiting for the phone to ring,
the hurricane coming closer and closer.
Days of wondering, How will I tell my daughter?
Waiting and waiting, braced for landfall.

Idiosyncrasies of the Body

I'm the kind of woman
who never skips a meal,
who always takes the end seat
closest to the door.
I raise rashes on my skin,
scratching imaginary itches.
I've got one right now
behind my fleshy arm.

I never appear naked in front of anyone.
When I bathe, I always lock
the door, even though the house
is empty. In school I used to imagine
the classroom door bursting open in the middle
of biology, a madman running in, pointing his gun
directly at me, and saying,
Take off your clothes, all of them,
and when I looked horrified, he'd add,
Or I'll kill you.
I turned to my teacher, a woman
who could not save me, and I prayed
for death to come quickly.

I have bizarre dreams.
Last night my father returned
from being dead. Once more he entered
the bedroom at the lake house, slipped
through the door like Zeus,
and pulled off my towel.
He'd seen hundreds of naked women, he said,
my father who for years

every time I passed him opened
my blouse—his right
to see how things were growing,
and I was a cold fish, just like my mother.

I envy other women,
especially those who go into a sauna
in a strange place and, in front of strangers,
strip down naked, so easy in their bodies.
And now I'm the teacher
when the door bursts open and my father walks in,
points his bony finger at me,
and in his thunderous voice, says, *Strip!*
Or I'll kill the children, all of them.
I watch my father, like the ancient Titan,
devour the children.

I am unclean in my body.
The summer my mother left
my father forbid me to lock the bathroom door.
His house. His roof. He could enter
any door he wanted. June, July, August,
I did not bathe, not once.
Each day I went down to the lake
and walked into the water.

In fashion I am most comfortable
in turtlenecks. I keep my blouses buttoned high.
I have never walked naked
in front of a man, not my husband
or my lovers, and do not know
how it feels to be a goddess
in front of a man,
how to bring him to his knees.

The Bee Charmer

On the sunrise walk I take to improve
       my health and my attitude, something
              landed in my hair. I brushed it away,

              and it stung me, deeply and painfully,
       in the palm of my hand. Back home,
I complained to my lover, called bees

God's mistake, debunked the old myth:
       they won't bother us if we don't bother
              them. He tweezed the tiny stinger and

              reminded me of the honey we enjoy on
       muffins. I said I'd switch to jelly if all bees
disappeared. He kissed my palm, sucked

out the poison, and brewed me a cup
       of jasmine tea, stirred with a dollop
              of honey. It tasted like nectar. Later my

              lover walked to the store, brought back
       the morning paper, a bag of honey buns,
and a fistful of yellow roses. He pointed

to the pollen inside the buds and
       rehearsed the necessity of bees,
              then kissed me until I surrendered—

              Okay, okay, some of the bees
       can stay. For hours, he hovered
over me. I felt the flutter of wings,

heard a buzz at my ear. I awoke
in noontime sunlight, my body
covered with the dusty bloom of pollen.

His Two Arms

dangle,
one on each side of his body
as he stands before the refrigerator,
leans in, and pillages for food—
purple grapes, a hunk
of Swiss, Kalamata olives—
his forearms covered
with a modicum of hair,
not ape-like but manly,
each of his arms
unadorned and no-nonsense,
muscled at the biceps,
not bulging and rippling and knotted
with blue veins
like on guys who pump iron
and wear tank shirts from Gold's Gym,
but curving and rising
like two hills bordering the campsite
where before you a feast is laid.

Pyromania

The heart wants what the heart wants,
and what it wants is fire.
My friend Roz, six months into a relationship
with a seemly man, dumps him
and says, *There's no fireworks.*
Roz wants the full-scale Grucci display—
her lover a licensed pyrotechnician,
Roman candles manually fired,
multi-color scenes, a barrage
of illuminations, the sky pulsing,
and always the Grand Finale.

Think of that woman in Colorado,
a forest ranger, who goes into the woods,
a letter from her estranged husband
clutched in her fist, a firestorm in her heart.
She reads the letter one last time,
strikes a match and kindles his words,
watches them shrivel.
Think of the entire forest in flames,
the blaze billowing and consuming,
trees surrendering to fire,
skeletons of timber, and charred remains.

And now I learn that silicone in the breasts
must be excised before cremation
or it blows up, liquefying to a dangerous substance,
destroying the crematorium.
I'd like to have breasts like that—
round and full, earth-tipped and tilted
heavenward, the kind that ignite and explode.

I'd like my breasts to burst into flame,
spreading like wildfire,
tongues of scarlet licking the walls.
I'd like breasts just that white-hot
as once they were under the touch
of my lover, so recently departed.
I'd like to burn the crematorium down.

About the Author

Diane Lockward is the author of two previous collections of poetry, *Eve's Red Dress* (Wind Publications, 2003) and a chapbook, *Against Perfection* (Poets Forum Press, 1998). Her poems have appeared in such journals as *Spoon River Poetry Review, The Beloit Poetry Journal,* and *Prairie Schooner,* as well as in several anthologies, including *Poetry Daily: 366 Poems from the World's Most Popular Poetry Website* and *Good Poems for Hard Times.* Her work has been featured on *Poetry Daily* and *Verse Daily* and read by Garrison Keillor on NPR's *The Writer's Almanac.* She is the recipient of a Poetry Fellowship from the New Jersey State Council on the Arts, several Pushcart Prize nominations, and awards from *North American Review, Louisiana Literature,* and the St. Louis Poetry Center. A former high school English teacher, she works as a poet-in-the-schools for both the New Jersey State Council on the Arts and the Geraldine R. Dodge Foundation. She lives in northern New Jersey.

Printed in the United States
60909LVS00002B/1-30

9 781893 239579